DENISE BRYSON

THE SEX
#I am better than this -

THE LIES
#WHEN SILENCE SPEAKS WHAT WILL IT SAY -

THE SOUL TIES
#BROKEN CHAINS TO FREEDOM

The Sex
#Iambetterthanthis

The Lies
#WhenSlienceSpeaksWhatWillItSay

The Soul Ties
#brokenchainstofreedom

Short Stories Poetically Infused

DENISE BRYSON

Copyright © December 28, 2020, by Denise Bryson

All rights reserved. No part of this publication may be reproduced, distributed, or transmitted in any form or by any means, including photocopying, recording, or other electronic or mechanical methods, without the prior written permission of the publisher, except in the case of brief quotations embodied in critical reviews and certain other noncommercial uses permitted by copyright law. For permission requests, write to the publisher, addressed "Attention: Permissions Coordinator," at the address below.

ISBN: 978-1-7351308-2-8 (Paperback)
ISBN: 978-1-7351308-3-50 (ePub)

Any references to historical events, real people, or real places are used fictitiously. Names, characters, and places are products of the author's imagination.

Front cover image by Artist. Rose Miller
Book design by Designer. Rose Miller
Printed, in the United States of America.
First printing edition 2021.

Afflatus Publishing
P.O. Box .2166
Desoto, TX 75123
www.AfflatusMerchandise.com

Table of Contents

Introduction 7

SECTION I: The Sex

A Seed Sown 10

Behavior Development 12

Caught Up 15

Celibacy 18

Confused, but Trusting You! 19

Exposure 21

Willing to Do 24

High Standards 26

I Told You I Was a Christian 28

I Want a Husband 30

If It Meant Nothing 32

Male Abstinence 34

MasterB 35

Mental Affair 38

My Sexuality 41

Reality Sex 43

Sex and the Single Saint 47

The Night Deposit 49
The Unmet Need 51
When I Was a Boy 55
When Sex Leads the Conversation 57
You Are Better Than That!!! 59

SECTION II: The Lies
A Secret, a Lie, Who Am I 62
Desperate for Love 64
Following Unforgiveness 66
I Gave 69
My Game 70
A Plot to Get the Twat 72
Secrets 74
When Silence Speaks 77
The Side Chick's Friend 79
These Men 80
These Scandals 81
What Did I Do? 83
While the Wife's Away 85
What Silence Uncovers 87

SECTION III: The Soul Ties
Abstinence—My Body Armor 91
Back to a Virgin's State of Mind 93

Did You Ask 95
I Know 97
I Was Designed to Be a Helpmeet 98
This Level of Pain 100
My Dignity 102
Not Yours 103
This Mess 105
Vices 108
God Filled the Empty Places 110
What Was Allowed 113
Seductive 115
You Chose Him 118
Broken Chains 119

Introduction

The Sex, the Lies, and the Soul Ties are short stories written with a poetic expression. The purpose of this book is to discuss unfortunate situations that affect people in different ways.

Some of these story typologies may affect how a person views, gives and receives love, especially those who have given up on real love.

Some instances have caused people to journey down pathways that were never their choice for life.

Section I of this book depicts life scenarios that, for some people, wishes would have never been fulfilled, but we want them to know that they are better than the unfortunate circumstances that envelope their life.

Sex has the power to unite. However, God was aware of the power that this act possessed, so he intended it to be enjoyed in the ties of marriage. However, love has been turned to lust. The lust for sex has been masked as sexual freedom; it has caused bondage, heartache, and grief. God created sex for intimacy. Sex is to celebrate love, to bring forth children into a family union. The pleasure of sex was supposed to be protected by the commitment of marriage.

These lustful acts of sexual freedom have united or tied people to each other, whether it was their intent or not. The fact that there was no intention of ever committing to each other, in some instances, has caused that sexual freedom to become silent moments in the lives of innocent and unwilling, and some willing participants. Its power has caused silent pain that people are holding, while they desire to be free but afraid to release the tragedy that invaded their innocence and bodies.

Section II -The Lies, what will silence say when it speaks of the pain caused, and the secrets kept? What will the broken silence unveil; what or who will it expose when it utters its words into the atmosphere so that the secret keeper can now be free. While praying, when we tell everything to God, we can tell our secrets, and he will guide us on how we should proceed in breaking our silence.

He will bring forth our healing in our willingness to forgive those who have hurt us discreetly.

Section III -The Soul Ties that have been created because of the lust of sex can be broken. Through the freedom that Christ has granted us through his sacrifice on the Cross. Galatians 5:1 ESV Bible "For freedom, Christ has set us free; stand firm therefore, and do not submit again to a yoke of bondage." As one begins to let go of the acts that created the soul tie and turn to God for help, one will forgive and become stronger. One day, they will say the chain is broken, and right now, I am free. These declarations can be uttered— "I am better than the lust of sex. I am no longer living in silence and the chains that once caused bondage has been broken. Let freedom, let deliverance ring."

The Sex

#I am better than this

I

A Seed Sown

I know sex is important to you

Sex is what you live and breathe

It would be best if you were more careful where you sowed your seed!

Every release you make is SEED-BEARING.

So, it should matter with whom you are sharing.

Sex is much more than the pleasure it brings

The climactic of an organismic joy

No sex should not be played with like a toy.

So, stop playing with the minds of women like little boys play with video games.

We are not a pair of Air Jordan's that you jump up and down in on the basketball court.

An exchange is taking place.

Just remember, whether it produces anything or not, a seed has been sown.

If sex is so important

Then why is the ground you are planting your seed in not critical?

Your seed was created to bring about life, not brokenness, abandonment, despair, and surely not bastards.

So, if sex is so important to you, where you plant your seed should be too!

2

Behavior Development

Mom and Dad, why didn't you protect me?

It was your responsibility.

Yet, the church members, not I, became your priority.

Yet, you scolded me often and shouted about my rebellion.

Maybe it would be different had you protected me.

Others brought their children, and you listened attentively to them, offering wise counsel and a possible solution.

Yet, for me, it seemed that no time was permitted.

Yet, you shouted aloud of my rebellion and sexual escapades.

You thought my sexual behavior was that of a harlot.

No, this behavior was developed from a seed planted when I was incredibly young.

The repeated offense came time after time by someone that you thought was so dear.

My silence incubated this seed, and it did grow into this sexual complication that has blossomed as a branch on my life's tree.

I wanted to be like you, Mom.

I wanted to give myself only to one man.

But that dream was shattered and taken from me when you repeatedly invited these monsters into our home.

I was always left alone with them.

Why? Because they were family.

Because you held them in such high esteem, I stayed in constant fear.

So, I kept silent.

Most of the time, when I talked, you assumed I was telling a lie.

That's another habit that I picked up by hearing lies told over and over again.

So, since I thought that you would not believe me, I kept silent.

My silence and their penetration developed this behavior.

It is funny we could talk about school, church, and everything else.

But this sexual conversation seemed to be taboo as if you were unaware that sex could happen.

You seemed to think that I was not born with the body parts or the desire to have sex.

Neither could you believe that I was a child progressing into a young woman and that I would encounter this aspect of life's experience?

But I did!

Repeatedly, I experienced this with family members.

Yes, family members!

Incest brought this behavior into existence.

So, when you think about this harlot behavior that you claim is me.

Your lack of protection and unwillingness to discuss the taboo elements that life can bring is what aided in this development.

My body's invasion, coupled with my silence, developed this, what I now call my being.

3

Caught Up

Caught up in the passion of love

Enticed by good loving

Made you think something good was coming out of that oven.

Caught up in the passion of love

Enticed by good loving

Had you in a daze

Wondering around like you were in a maze.

Not thinking clearly about the fact that what she was feeding you was restaurant-purchased food.

Masked as home cooking

You did not know that girl could not cook?

Caught up in the passion of love

Entranced by exceptional looks

Made you think that girl was keeping

A balanced checkbook.

Then you run into that good girl you passed by
You see her and take a deep breath and sigh.
Wondering what could have been
Had you not allowed seduction to suck you in.

Then you came to yourself.
You realized nothing good ever came out of that oven.
That house was never clean unless you cleaned it.

The worst of it all
Your money took a fall.
All because you were caught up in the passion of love
Entranced in her exceptional looks
Excited by that freak in the bed.

So, listen as wisdom speaks.
Next time
Calm the raging beast
Put the loving on hold.
Open your eyes wide so that you can see how seduction is living.
Who seduction is behind the mask of fancy living
Observe those spending habits

Listen to what she is communicating.

Listen to what seduction is asking of you.

Before you put a ring on it and head to the altar to say I DO!!!

4

Celibacy

Celibacy does not mean that there is no desire.

It means I have chosen to remain untouched.

Abstinence does not mean that the urge does not rise with a need to be satisfied.

It means that I have chosen not to satisfy the flesh I live in.

Celibacy does not mean that I do not crave the desire to be embraced.

It means that I do not chase it; I don't give in to it.

Celibacy—the choice to do it God's way.

5

Confused, but Trusting You!

Lord God, I have made a conscious effort to do it your way

No sex until I am married

Yet, I am still single.

I see my friends diving in

Doing what the world terms doing what grown folks do.

Yet they have received a ring.

Walked the aisle, celebrated the wedding day, enjoyed the honeymoon.

How did the sinful way get rewarded?

While the godly way suffers loneliness?

I am confused

Not one, not two, but three and more have received the blessing of marriage.

Yet, I still sit lonely while I celebrate with them genuinely.

Holding on to what Your word says, "Take delight in the LORD, and he will give you your heart's desires." NLT

Yet, to the human eye, this way seems dead.

Nevertheless, I will continue God with Your way.

I know that I will receive the reward of my desire someday.

I am trusting in You God, no matter what it looks like

Your approach is best for me, regardless of what my eyes see.

My prayer, you do hear.

I am one of your dears.

Life at times seems so confusing; however, God, I trust you.

6

Exposure

Why am I this way, exposure?

Why do I crave the fruit that is forbidden?

My urges I can no longer keep hidden.

Why am I this way, exposure?

Why do I seek sex without commitment exposure?

What I was exposed to fuels what I desire.

This is not what I envisioned for my life.

But your sexual misconduct exposed me.

Exposed me to sexual promiscuity

I did not seek this life on my own; I was exposed.

Hiring me out to the men, you would entertain for money.

We all had to work, is what you would say.

I experienced the pain day after day.

I acted out in school, which then labeled me as a troubled teen.

If I speak one word to anybody, you told me that our family will be torn apart and that it will be my fault.

Of course, this was the lie you told all four of us, your girls.

You dressed me up night after night to their delight.

Every time I wanted to die,

Yet, time and time again, you dressed me then hired me out.

Like a call girl, yet not a dime did I see as you said everybody had to work.

Even the dogs you would breed and sell their pups.

Though all the money went to keep a roof over our head and keep you looking fabulous,

While you set and slept resting as you say

Your hard work was pimping us out.

What a monster you are, not a mother.

Monster mom, you only love yourself, not us, so my position is that of an employee, not your daughter.

Please stop being offended that my sisters and I do not bring our kids around to meet you.

You will not use another generation for your lewd behavior.

Bye, mother, I do forgive you, but I will not visit you, nor will my children.

Jesus found me, and I introduced my siblings to Him, as well.

So, He loves us unconditionally, and we have been healed from the scars you gave us.

But before I go, I want you to know that Jesus loves you too!!!

Despite what you did to us, if you surrender to Him and let Him into your heart,

You will experience love like you never felt before.

So, let me expose you to a man who will not play with you but save you.

Let Jesus into your heart. He will come and stay.

See you through all of life's difficulties, deliver you, make you new, forgive you, accept you, and love you unconditionally.

Mother, he died for you too on the cross.

So mother, ask Him into your heart and experience the healing that we all have experienced.

Jesus loves you too, yes, even you.

7

Willing to Do

What am I willing to do for love?

To feel like I am adored

This waiting game is boring

I need a man now

So, I give myself willingly

Hoping for love to arise and embrace me

Week after week, a loving man I seek

Yet, they enjoy my free lunch.

Yet, no one will buy the goods.

They turn me every which way having all access.

Deposit after deposit, they make

Yet they continue to withdraw

No one stays in the bank vault.

My body feels like used goods.

I tell myself that I am adored; look how many want me.

Just like High School, I was a popular girl.

Yet, no one wanted to be seen with me.

I was a joke full of lies and smoke.

Not a real fire to be desired

What I have been willing to do for the feeling of love.

What I need to do for love is to accept the love of God.

God is love! Only when I am willing to experience His love will I know what real love is.

8

High Standards

You tell me my standards are too high.

How can I live up to your expectation?

And you wonder why you are still single.

Well, I do not believe that I am to blame.

I was spoiled by my father, who lived the definition of a provider in life and death.

You see, he worked to make sure he provided for his family.

He loved me unconditionally.

Told me how beautiful I am.

So, I expect the same from whoever wants to be my man, my husband.

My brother followed in his footsteps and learned to be a provider and encourager.

When we were with him, he took care of the bill.

So once again, I have been spoiled by their actions, their love.

Now, my male friends take good care of me.

They open doors, pull out chairs, sometimes get the check,

Celebrate birthdays with me

Call to check on me to see if I am safe.

We can communicate about anything.

Watches out and protects me

These actions have been going on since I was a little girl.

So yes, my standards are high.

They listen when I need an ear.

Then God is always taking care of me.

He told me that he fearfully and wonderfully made me,

Loves me unconditionally.

He is my divine protection.

My Provider

My Everything

So yes, my standards are high.

He told me that the man that comes into my life should love me like Christ loves the church.

So yes, my standards are high.

9

I Told You I Was a Christian

I told you I was a Christian

However, that word means nothing to you.

I know you feel that the words I am a Christian do not align with the actions of the one claiming to be

But for me, I try to live up to what my mouth proclaims I am a Christian.

One of God's girls

The apple of his eye

A Christian.

You seem to like that about me but

Your pursuit of my fruit is mind-boggling.

Because it says to me that you think I am a liar

That what I profess I do not possess.

My desire to be a true Christian sets me apart.

So, you continue to pursue my forbidden fruit that has been set aside for my husband.

Your conversation used in my ear is like predatory sexual tactics.

I told you I was a Christian deciding to live God's way.

I know you hear a lot of women say it but then do not live it.

But I am not that woman.

For you to try to challenge me with your sexual innuendo, saying I want to make love to you.

Like I am too stupid to translate that this is the pursuit of a one-night stand or, for you, another woman added to your sexual rotation parade.

By now, the offense is settling in.

I am trying to keep my old nature from rising.

So that you will not experience words that will be demising to you.

Can you please stop and change the conversation and let us move on?

Before the old me you will have to see?

You have been forewarned.

But your mind is blocked.

You continue your plot to get the twat.

But I am assuring you that you will not be getting any.

I will not be another notch in your mind of many.

Right now, I am listening to the Holy Spirits leading.

To get up immediately from this table.

Before I decide to ignore my way of escape provided

Letting the old me arise from being buried under the blood of Jesus

So, I must go so that you will know.

That when I say I am a Christian.

I mean just that, I am a Christian.

10

I Want a Husband

Yes, I want a husband.

But I do not, want yours.

I want one free and clear.

So, when he says to me, dear.

I know that it is me he is referring to

He is not mistakenly having thoughts of you.

His #1.

Yes, I want a single man who is a husband.

Not just any ole man but a husband

I want a God-fearing man.

A man free to be with me.

I do not want a man that is wandering from one woman to another.

A man that is free and ready to be committed.

Yes, I want a man who is already a husband before he finds a wife.

One free and clear

Not committed by a marriage license

Not committed on paper while appearing free

While your game is strong, your pursuit is wrong.

So yes, I want a husband.

Just not a man, especially not an adulterer

These titles may be the banner you are standing under

However, I want a man/husband looking for a wife, not a playmate or a concubine.

I want a man who wants to be a husband looking for a wife so the two can become one.

I know my friend; you think to yourself if she knew what you know.

I would not make this declaration or pray this prayer.

However, please try not to destroy my dreams by talking to me about wanting a husband.

Because your experience was horrible

Yes, I want a man, a God-fearing man.

A man living for God and God's purpose

There are good men still existing, so I will keep believing.

God has a good man for me.

A man/husband saved, free, unattached, and willing to be committed.

11

If It Meant Nothing

Why did you engage in something?

That you said meant nothing?

If the one you absolutely love

Is the one you are with

Yet with another, you did slip.

Over and over and over again

However, to me, you say it meant nothing.

How long has this charade

Or might I ask has it been a parade?

Of nothings you say

Yet you were engaged every day.

When I met you, I thought I was enough?

To satisfy your desires.

For me, you seem to have such a fire.

Why did you touch the thigh?

Evidently, the touch made you high.

For another hit,

Now you cannot quit.

You say you love me

But your desire is she.

You say it meant nothing.

As you repeat the offense.

You think simply to repent.

That you repenting will repair all my disparity.

Yet, you continue to make deposits like it is a charity.

You say it meant nothing.

But nothing has been going on and on for a long time.

Now out of the blue, a baby is born.

Yet you still say it meant nothing.

12

Male Abstinence

I have decided to abstain.

Yet you question if I can.

I am a man, and I have decided to refrain.

Yes, from sex.

You shout, how can this be

A man has needs.

Christ did it. He was both God and Man.

He is my example.

Yes, I am a man with God's Holy Spirit living inside me.

His Holy Spirit gives me the power to abstain.

So, you can doubt all you want

I have made my decision.

No matter what you believe

It is difficult, but not impossible.

Yes, this man has decided to abstain from sex.

13

MasterB

Is touching oneself privately really a sin?

Then why does the urge come again and again?

The exploration of self-gratification is wrong too?

If I do not explore, how will I know what I adore?

How will I tell my spouse to be what pleasures me if I don't know?

All because I was afraid to explore

Because someone determined it was a sin.

Why was I created with this desire, this burning fire?

If it is a sin to satisfy this feeling

What do I use to extinguish the fire?

I pray and pray it works for a while

The thoughts don't go away for long.

Something in life will trigger the song to replay.

Do I run out of every store that plays love songs?

Do I shy away from every movie that displays love scenes?

Do I shy away from conversations that trigger this emotion?

Do I continue to appear unresponsive to these emotions publicly?

While I cry privately from the disparity of no intimacy

I chose to masturbate, thinking that this was my only choice.

Since hooking up is a sin while being single.

Masturbation appears to be a single act, but is it?

Am I reacting off of a memory of being with someone?

Am I reacting from a visual I have seen?

Or, am I channeling a thought of someone I would like to have an intimate relationship with?

Imagine what it would be if we could come together.

So, is masturbation a solo act?

If not, then how do we explain a young boy or girl that has no memory to recall

Yet, when puberty strikes, these hormones rage and begin their fight.

Physically it is only one person doing the deed by hand or device.

Mentally, it is an imagination of hookups.

A physical exploration acted out to come to this orgasmic conclusion.

Satisfied, gratified, orgasm(s) achieved

How can this be a sin too?

I guess since we are born into sin and shaped in iniquity.

The desire comes from the seed of sin surfaces again and again.

So, I have to make a choice time and time again.

Not to participate in this sin.

The more I resist, the strong man is weakened.

Soon my resistance will cause him to flee.

The victory over this act can be achieved. It is up to me.

I can win this battle.

He promised me a way to escape.

Listen to the direction in which God gives so escape can be achieved.

Yes, there is a way out of every situation.

Listen and follow His lead.

With Jesus, I can find the way out.

Begin to live victoriously day in and day out.

14

Mental Affair

One thinks no physical action means no sin.

Oh, how you have been deceived again

Texting is harmless.

The pictures are too.

However, the recipient of them is not your Boo.

They belong to someone else.

Your thoughts of them

If played out would be very grim.

Your spouse trusts you to be faithful.

You think I have not committed the act.

But you imagine this person laying on their back.

Don't you know you are having a mental affair?

You imagine what you would do if you did not already have a Boo.

Yet you do not know that you are having a psychological affair.

When you gaze upon their body, the one they sent at your request. You think it is innocent because you are not touching.

However, as you gaze upon their picture, the lust for them arises, the mind begins to go to that place, and if you are not careful, your body will begin its chase of gratification, so yes, it is wrong; it is called a mental affair.

Your request, if uncovered, will find you in an outright mess.

They belong to someone else no matter what their status.

Again, I say, don't you know you are having a mental affair?

When you gaze upon them, wanting them

Understand me; you have just committed a sin.

Lusting is the term given.

So, yes, in sin, you are living.

You scream in your defense, "I have not slept with anyone."

But in your mind, you have had sex many times.

Your intentions want them bad.

Not knowing you are betraying the trust is oh so sad.

Your affair may not be physical, so there is no evidence of it.

Your intentions, your mental venture allows you to relive it.

Having a mental affair is the same betrayal Jesus himself stated if you look on a woman to commit adultery, you have sinned in your heart.

Thinking it is innocent, no harm, no foul.

Once again, you are deceived.

The bottom line is you desire to have sex with someone other than your spouse.

Though not physically acted upon is still adultery.

It's a mental affair.

If the act is wrong, so are the intentions.

Being faithful with your body but not your mind is still broken vital trust.

Trust is a mixture of the foundation of marriage.

When it is broken, the foundation begins to crack.

Having an interest in the opposite sex is natural.

But you are filling your head repeatedly with fantasies.

You are having a mental affair.

15

My Sexuality

Because I do not desire your twat

My sexuality is in question.

He must be gay

What man can resist all this?

They all should, with the way you offer it up!!!

But I will, I do, resist your twat

It has nothing to do with my desire for the opposite sex.

It has everything to do with how you present yourself as a woman.

I am the hunter, not the hunted.

I pursue.

Me not pursuing you does not declare that there is something wrong with me.

I make good choices

Your promiscuous ways, I will have nothing to do with

I deserve better than that.

God told Hosea to marry a harlot.

He has not spoken that to me.

I know you were not the rib taken from my side.

So, me not wanting you has nothing to do with my sexuality.

But it does have to do with the standard of my choice.

16

Reality Sex

Your touch is so endearing.
The warmth I feel is somewhat fearing.
It makes me think that this could go somewhere.
So, I sit and imagine with this blank stare.
Gazing afar off.

I know you said I just like making love to you.
No commitment will I do.
Just let me make love to you.

Once again, as I feel the warmth of your embrace.
It sends my mind to an intimate place.
Wondering why it will never be more
You make love to me as you adore.

Wow!! How can this be
Where do you go in your mind when you touch me?

How can this be a drive-by sex encounter masked as making love?
You say I have never treated you like a drive-by sex encounter.
Never knowing every time we come together, I fall.
So yes, no commitment + lovemaking = a drive-by sex encounter.

Deeper in an emotional web
Caught in this thing in my bed.
It is incredible how I have never seen your place.
You say it exists, just not for me face to face.
I often wonder if I am on rotation.
A different one each week is your situation.

I cannot understand why you drink the milk but will not buy
I know I just wanted to have some fun.
But every time you have touched me, I became undone.
Unraveling my emotions for you
Now there is a soul tie.
Freely, I gave myself I cannot lie.
Now I am in so deep
My thoughts of you I can't keep
Hidden any longer
Each day they keep getting stronger.
No matter what I say or do

You keep being you.

Stating I want to make love to you

That is the sound I hear.

Your actions make it sound so dear.

The reality is, no matter what you say, it is.

The fact mirrors a drive-by sex encounter; that is what it is.

So how long will one allow this lovemaking drive-by sex encounter to continue?

His hands all on you, his private parts inside you

Depositing more of himself in you

Putting it in but drawing nothing out.

When God instituted this for marriage

The deposit would always come with a withdrawal.

The connection would create oneness, the two becoming one.

The deposit was to form a seed that would blossom into a little one.

What does one do to get back to who God made them to be?

Stop the affair!

The single saint is married to God until his or her mate comes.

Intimacy without marriage is an act of fornication, period.

Stop making excuses and get serious.

You are more than a depository.

Stop letting him in; change your story.

The outcome is up to you.

With Jesus' help, you can do it.

Yeah, it will be hard at first.

The love of Jesus Christ can give you the burst of healing you need

Breaking the soul tie

Tell him bye, bye

It is OK to go ahead and cry.

You will survive

Go ahead shout aloud, giving praise for your freedom today.

17

Sex and the Single Saint

Sex for the single saint according to God's design is a no, no

But for some, their heart says engage; who will know.

Sex for me, I cannot enjoy

This inner voice that speaks loudly, continuing to annoy.

As I lay there, going through the motion

A voice in my head says you should not be doing this.

There was nothing wrong with either party.

However, for me, I cannot relax enough to enjoy myself.

For fear of what I am engaged in is against God's will;

Therefore, I lay there, and I think to myself, why am I here?

The person I am with is so dear.

However, I cannot enjoy this display of lust-love

Because for me, it's not love without marriage; my values kick in.

So, as I lay there not into what is going on, I think to myself.

These actions are pointless; why go through the agony of defeat.

When if I wait for marriage, will this be a sweet treat?

Therefore, sex and single saints do not mix.

Because if God is your father, the sin makes you feel happy then sick.

Sex God gave it as a gift under the marriage commitment.

It is a pleasure of sexual intimacy that brings an emotional connection.

The Bible reference is the man knew his wife, the two coming together, body, soul, and spirit becoming one.

Singles having sex is the sin committed within, against their own body.

Yes, God created sex to be fun, but for us to be good stewards and enjoy.

Even when single at the moment, it can feel amazing.

When the high wears off, the guilt starts blazing.

Your mind begins to ask the question, why do I allow

Them to drink the milk and not buy the cow.

Sex is a reflection of God's loving goodness.

God created sex not to be dirty or shameful if done his way.

Sexual sin where one has been sinned against, God does not hold you accountable.

Let his love free your mind of the insurmountable guilt, and shame let God heal the pain.

God wants us to reserve sex for marriage then it will be loving, enjoyable, and guilt-free.

So, wait for the blessing of marriage.

Then will sex be the enjoyment that God intended for it to be.

18

The Night Deposit

You are so proud of your member

That you think I should surrender

To your request to make love.

When we both know that the word commitment is not in your vocabulary

Nor is it apart of your character.

You think that just because I do not fall into the size 2 to 12 category.

That I should feel privileged because you are willing to make love, you say to me.

But only in the dark

So, you will not have to see the real me, with all my imperfections as your mind perceives.

Only in the dark

So, you will not have to see my face.

As you get up and leave in the night

Because your love maker does not want to wake up next to me.

Yet you think I should feel privileged.

Because you asked me to make your night drop in my body.

Pull in to drop your night deposit, then drive off in the dark.

You think that I should feel privileged because you have asked this of me.

I am worth too much to bow to your request.

Too Blessed to be your in-the-dark whore.

Keep moving; you are handsome but not that handsome.

For me to deny the ransom paid for me.

His name is Jesus; yes, He paid the price for my freedom, yes for me

So, I will not be your night deposit.

19

The Unmet Need

My need for sex and your desire to fulfill

Do not seem to be in sync.

My loving desire to please you, my dear

Appears to be unimportant to you.

Nevertheless, you enjoy it when I do what I do.

I desire the taste of you.

It makes my adrenaline burn like fire.

Yet you, for me, is drenched with an unwillingness to fulfill my need.

You wonder why my eye wonders, up and down another woman's thigh.

Wishing and wondering with a sigh, of how it would be to be involved with someone that wants it and gives it just like me.

Your constant rejection of my hunger, my fire

Is what is changing my desire?

For what you give and for where I live

You treat me like my meat is not a grade-A prime cut.

You reject it like it is contaminated when I ask for you to treat it like your favorite lollipop with a delight in the center or your favorite ice-cream flavor on a waffle cone.

Your intimacy runs and hides after you get your orgasmic high

Then you wonder why I seek a chick on the side.

I thought when I said I do that in every way; we would please each other.

I guess you wanted the ring more than the thing.

You went along for a while

Then the lovemaking changed with each child.

I know when you fake with your moans.

Even the orgasm shake is fake.

Are you that selfish to think I cannot tell?

I hear other husbands talk about how their wives seek ways to please them.

I sit in silence because I do not have a pleasurable detail to share

I sit there in jealous despair.

I want to be faithful only to you; that was why to you at the altar I said, I do.

What do I do, sit, and become bitter because I am in this thing called marriage?

I am married to someone who is too selfish to meet my needs.

But always wants their needs met?

Do I cheat and hope I do not get caught?

End the marriage based on the desire of my little head

Suck it up and deal with the fact that for me, the intimacy is dead.

Maybe just one time, I will seek to see

How it will be with another who wants a good man

Someone to hold her hand, treat her nice.

So, another I seek

With her, I can unleash the sexual beast within

Although I know it is a sin.

When I am with her, she fulfills all my fantasies without hesitation.

She appreciates what you have but will not please.

So, she does what you should do to me.

With her, I get to shiver and quake.

Please make no mistake; none of her actions are fake.

So, since she gives me her best

I give her my best; her response to me is real.

Because of that, I am a repeat offender.

What is interesting is that you are too selfish even to realize the decline in our bedroom.

Too selfish to know I no longer ask you to assume the position.

I guess you are relieved and think that my sex drive has diminished.

Yeah, but I give you what you want and let you have your fun when you want to.

Then I go for a run and get what I need from another.

I know you think you are my 80%

What is so beautiful about this diamond that I found?

This woman in the 80 percentile?

I heard the women's department leader tell you, girls, at Church that what you will not do, another will.

I guess you missed that useful information.

Or you decided to ignore it and keep doing marriage your way.

Men need sex

It is important to us.

So, you continue doing what you will not do.

When the divorce papers come and are served to you

Do not cuss, do not fuss, and please do not call me all kinds of names.

Just reflect on what you decided not to do

Understanding who you just let walk away.

She was not looking for me, unlike you.

This one I found, and to her, I will say I do.

Since I believe in marriage

The joy it brings

How you are to please me.

I am to love you as Christ loved the Church.

I admit to the mistake I made of marrying you.

You gave it to me as Eve gave to Adam.

I accepted then, but I am rejecting now.

I hope one day you can forgive me.

For what is currently happening

The papers are being served.

We will soon be free to get our needs met.

You will no longer have to deal with me, nor I, you.

Today we are free to be happy and fulfilled.

20

When I Was a Boy

When I was a boy, you took advantage of me

pinned me down because you were stronger than me.

Entered a place inside me where you had no right to be

You took advantage of me.

I was so young when this happened; I had no strength to fight

So, you used your power and might and took advantage of me.

You were supposed to teach me how to be a man

Instead, you took my manhood away with your perversion.

I knew this was not supposed to be, but you kept on entering me

Yes, you took advantage of me.

I was not sure at the time why I was your target

I later discovered that boys were your choice.

You only pretended to want women, while I possessed the same parts as you

So, that was your desire, the perversion that fueled your fire

Yes, you took advantage of me.

I hated every time my mother left for work because I knew you would enter my room.

I tried to tell her, but you threatened to kill her if I did, and you told me to be brave and take it.

I was a young boy and what you were doing to me had nothing to do with being a man or being brave.

The pain I felt each time was so intense I wanted to die so that you would stop.

The shame that you caused me made me withdraw from others.

Now you have the nerves to call me names and make fun of my actions.

When your perversion has caused this behavior

Yes, you, my stepfather, you took advantage of me.

Sometimes I blame my mother for marrying you.

Her desperation to not be ashamed of having a baby and no husband

It caused her to accept your proposal before knowing who you were.

So, night after night, I suffered the pain and the shame of your perversion.

Yes, you took advantage of me.

21

When Sex Leads the Conversation

Too dense to know that when sex leads the conversation, my mind immediately shuts you out.

I just met you, yet sex leads the conversation!

In my mind, I move on immediately when sex leads the conversation.

If all I want is sex with no emotion, no commitment, and no love, I can order something online for non-emotional and no love sex.

It will be loyal if the batteries are good and drama free.

Your sex lead conversation says to me you are not faithful, and all you want is to see if I am willing to be drawn into this web of sexual immorality.

Your conversation lets me know that you are still a young man with raging hormones, not ready for a real relationship, and certainly, not mentally equipped for anything short-term and indeed not long-term.

Your conversation is still that of a young man powered by hormones.

When you become a man, your conversation will be different.

Although your hormones will still rage, the hormones you will control with Godly wisdom on how to approach a Godly woman.

You will not bring sex to the stage to make it the leading man.

You will let it make its entrance if this relationship is going somewhere.

But in the beginning, you would not dare

Lead the conversation with that junk.

Men, when sex leads the conversation, and we have just met.

Real women, although physically still in the room, leave the room mentally.

22

You Are Better Than That!!!

You are better than that.

Stop being picked up and put down like a baseball bat.

Letting them use your body to hit home runs

Causing your emotions to unravel, becoming undone.

You are better than that!

A different man every week for free

Yet you judge the woman that charges a fee.

When she uses her body to swing and hit

She costs top dollar for every lick they get

But you look down at her.

She is a businesswoman.

She gets paid for what she does.

However, you are a cheap imitation.

You are willing to do the same for free.

Yet, you judge her because she charges a fee.

The girl on the pole works for tips

Yet you judge her and call her a stank hoe.

But you do the same for free.

Freak is what they call you.

A coochie call is a drive-by stop they make frequently.

Yet you feel superior to those who get paid.

You look down on them as if what you are doing is better.

When the fact is, you too should be wearing a Scarlett Letter.

So, stop and think before you continue to sink.

Realize you are better than a free imitation of a call girl

You have to know your worth

You were fearfully and wonderfully made.

You need to come clean to yourself and stop the cheap imitation of a no fee-based call girl.

Understand your worth

Increase your self-esteem

And know that you are better than that.

The LIES

#When silence speaks what will it say

23

A Secret, a Lie, Who Am I

A secret, a lie, who am I

The truth has been revealed

I am not your child.

The mother I always knew is my aunt.

Because my birth mother did not want me

The father I grew up knowing, I learned, is not my father.

The seed that was planted that developed to be me

I have no idea who sowed the seed.

I did not come from this man who I call dad.

So, I heed to say, "Who am I?"

My DNA is tied to people who did not want me.

The kept secret should have been shared a long time ago then I would know that my birth parents did not want me.

Now my life is on hold wondering, who I am

You thought you were doing the right thing.

But the pain that I feel lets me know that this secret, this lie was not right.

So now I am in an inward fight.

I am trying to take in this secret, this lie that you adults choose to hide.

This mess is tearing me up on the inside.

DNA no match,

Yes, I know you both love me as if I came out from you.

However, there are so many like me; it causes us to wonder who I am.

I took on your characteristics because I lived with you, but whose DNA do I have.

Although you have never treated me like I did not belong

Thank you for all the love you gave me unconditionally.

Yes, my parents, that is who you are to me.

I know that for sure you raised me.

However, I do wonder whose DNA I came from.

I wonder who am I?

24

Desperate for Love

So desperate for love

That second is OK

She would rather be second than not loved at all.

He is with her, but he loves me; she believes.

He states one day, she will be his number one.

While he goes home to her

He says I will be free soon.

She envisions that day like a full moon.

So, she will continue to give him what he wants.

Time after time

It has been a couple of years.

He assures her not to fear.

He will be free soon.

She envisions that day like a full moon.

When we are together, I imagine that I am his exclusively.

Yet, she sees the pictures he posts on his social media page.

Them walking hand in hand

She is looking like she is his woman.

He assures her it is complicated.

I love you, not her, he says

The only time we are hand in hand is in the bed-chamber, where no one can see

She is his private dancer.

If only he had known her before his wife

His life would be perfect, he states.

Yes, then he posts the picture of the new car he just purchased for her.

When all his #2 girl receives is the free breakfast at the place they meet.

Am I that desperate for love? She begins to think.

That I allow myself to be in this place pondering her life choices

He knows what to say, how, and how to make me feel.

When he touches her, her body gets a chill.

Yet he is not mine; he is hers as she remembers.

She is in a place called the desperation of loves façade

Well, she has been there before with the same outcome, "Used again."

Desperation is the blind spot of the reality of love as #2.

25

Following Unforgiveness

Sucked in by loneliness

Lured by the gentle touch of the tempting conversation

Her seductive moves, her soft voice, sweet smell

He just wanted intimacy.

An ear to hear

A voice to respond

A touch so dear

He did not want the whole deal.

But he was sucked in by loneliness.

Lured by the gentle touch of her

tempting conversation

Not realizing the consequences that lie in wait

All because of this obscure date

She looked fine, while all the time

She was full of disease

Given to her in this same type of date

By someone she thought would soon be her mate.

Because of her pain, she sought vengeance.

On whoever would answer her seductive call

She attempted to make him fall.

Into her clutches of bitterness

Brought by her fatal date

All he wanted was intimacy.

A kind ear to hear his cry.

He did not know that this meeting would turn his life around.

Turn his smile into a frown.

All because of her bitterness.

That day for her was all a big lie.

The results are causing her to die.

So, she becomes a seductive killer.

Using her pillow talk, her still intact looks.

She will lure them into her sin.

So, they can pay for that day.

She went on that date with a potential mate.

Now she cannot get rid of what he gave her.

She knows she is wrong, but her bitterness is affecting many.

How many will die because of her cry?

The mistake she made was not protecting herself with abstinence or latex.

It is not every man's fault.

But she cannot punish the person.

He is no longer breathing.

So instead of letting go and dealing with the choice she made

She allows her un-forgiveness to make her into a murder.

Instead of forgiving and becoming an ambassador for abstinence

She chose not to forgive and become

A cold-blooded killer

Where has un-forgiveness led you?

26

I Gave

I gave my body, yet you don't love me.

I laid it down next to you; however, you don't love me.

I made sure that I would do all that you wanted me to do, yet you don't love me.

You said you did when I withheld, only to find out later you don't love me.

It was only gestures, for winning the game to get it and quit it.

Now you say, "I am too attached; you need space."

When I withheld, I could not get you out of my face.

I was your baby, your lady; now that you got it, you are shady.

Now, I know you did not love me.

I was to fulfill your fantasy at the time.

I ask myself, why did I give in and commit this sin.

Was I so needing to be loved that I ignored the signs of the game?

Yes, I ignored them, acting insanely.

I thought your words, "I love you," were real.

Later, only to find out they were just a part of the hit and quit the sex and lies game deal.

Now I seek Jesus to heal, why because

I gave my body, and I gave my mind. I gave.

27

My Game

My game is to use my pretty to get what I want.

Yes, I am a user.

My game is to use my pretty to get what I want.

Lying to you about how I feel

She is lying to you about how you are the only one.

Man, you think you are playing a game with me.

You are, sadly, mistaken.

I am playing you

Your high paying job is what attracts me to you.

Yes, the six-figure income.

Your good looks are just a bonus.

I know that you have been hurt, and so have I

But this time, I am playing you.

Maybe one day I will love you.

But for now, these promises you are making are what attracts me to you.

Yes, my game is to do what I need to get you to keep you, and hopefully, one day, I will love you for you and not what you offer.

Sorry, but for now, this is my game.

My pretty is getting me what I want, and yes, right now, I am playing what I know to be my game.

28

A Plot to Get the Twat

He walked through the door, tall and fine

I begin to think he is mine.

He begins to wile me with his alluring words.

That start at my head and continue down my every curve.

"Wow," he admires me a lot, or he thinks I am a thot.

Then it hits me, girl! It is a plot to get the twat.

But I am mesmerized by what he is saying.

 I ignore the first warning and continue to bask.

In his seductive compliments of me

I thought to myself; he loves my every curve and the beauty I possess

If he keeps talking, I am sure to be in a mess.

He touches my hands, and he begins to say

"You are tense; let me massage it all away.

Just a little massage that is all,

I promise I will not touch anything else.

Unless you would let me eat a little dessert and satisfy my sweet tooth

Just looking at you, I know you are sweet, like a homemade peach cobbler warm with ice-cream on top.

A decadent dessert that if I get one taste, I will want to come back for more."

By now, your body is beginning to respond, and you feel yourself slipping into a bond.

Pondering the thought, and then you think to yourself.

A massage that would not hurt

He promises that it is all he will do

Unless I say have some desert

(Hello) what are you thinking?

Snap out of it; he has given you his best shot.

Girl, it is a plot to get the twat.

Make your journey out of wonderland.

And remember your motto, or have you forgot.

Girl, you must withhold the twat.

Do not fall for that plot, of fascinating words or whatnot.

Girl, if you do it God's way, you will withhold the twat.

You deserve more than a massage and to give away a slice of your dessert.

You want him to buy the whole thing, which is worth a lot.

A price that is far above rubies is what the Bible says.

So, shake yourself, do not give in to that deceiving plot.

Remember your worth, your commitment to God, and withhold, I mean to withhold the twat.

29

Secrets

These secrets that one keeps about themselves

Is this the reason that their life is stacked on a shelf lying dormant?

You could be free to live your promise.

But you chose the secret life instead.

The secret life is usually sinful.

But it feels like your living because you live in this dysfunction.

You promise yourself I am going to get my life off this shelf and live you say.

Then you struggle to keep your promise to yourself to change.

The experience comes with valleys that we must walkthrough.

So, we choose the secrets because they feel right for now.

It may be the status quo life, but I am not suffering like I see others.

I at least have a part of you.

Although it is a lie

But look at how I live.

Better than most, the things I get because of what I do for him

I would not have, so I would rather live like this.

Then live wanting, like I see others.

I will take being a secret.

It is better than being lonely and needy.

I know it is she he adores

He provides me this lifestyle, which means more to me.

Who wants to be broke and desperate? Not me.

So yes, his secret is what I will be

Letting him continue living happily with she

Yes, she gets all the praise for being his wife.

But I have a calm life living this secret and not causing strife.

Yes, I am his secret.

I know God disapproves.

I waited so long on a prayer to be answered.

But it never came, so I proclaim

God sent the answer it was not the one I wanted so,

I have accepted being his secret.

God help me to stay silent and not cause any mess.

It seems to be the best for me, the way you blessed

How this secret has me deceived

I know that is a twisted thought, God you have nothing to do with this arrangement.

I waited so long, for my Prayer I prayed, to have my own, to have and hold, Prayer never answered.

What was I to do? Keep waiting?

So, I helped you out.

I took what was before me.

I am happy it appears.

When I see you with she

Reality reminds me

I am living this secret.

30

When Silence Speaks

When Silence speaks, what will it say?

Will it tell about the sexual advances that were done to me that day?

Will it speak about how you hurt me over and over again?

You were a relative, but that day you became a predator to me.

Will it tell of the lies that you told me to tell?

That has caused me to be in this private hell.

I was locked up inside, like being sentenced to jail.

Will it tell of the soul tie that was formed that day and the many days after that?

How I begin to think you loved me in a bizarre way

Because at some time, the acts of incest begin to feel different

All because I gave in to this stimulating invasion.

When Silence speaks, what will it say?

Will it tell of the shame I feel when I see my aunt?

Knowing you were her husband, and yet, you found your way in my room often.

I came to live with you all because my parents could not keep me.

So, they sent my sister and me there with you both to give us a better life.

If they only knew what kind of life their decision gave us

What would they think?

My sister tried to tell them about the experience it brought to her.

My aunt and my mother blamed her and said it was her fault.

Now, I have not seen my sister in years.

She left to escape

We do not know if she is dead or alive.

All because of the predator I call uncle, my aunt's husband.

So, quiet, Silence, it is better if you do not speak.

No one is ready to believe you; he is a well-respected man in the community.

And you a troubled teen, so they think.

For seven years, this has been my secret.

So, quiet, Silence, you better not speak.

No, quiet, Silence, you will ruin it for everyone.

But I fear for my little girl, who is my uncle's daughter by incest.

I refuse to let this hell repeat.

So, my Silence, you must speak.

31

The Side Chick's Friend

The side chick's friend is privileged to the details.

Not really wanting to know, but a listening ear to hear is what the side chick needs.

To try to ease the pain felt for deeds she has done.

Although she paints the picture as if she is thrilled about the episodes of sexual encounters

So, she tells you of the conversations the acts of sexual pleasure.

All the while trying to feel unique to him

Then reality sets in, and the realization come front and center.

Making her realize I am the side chick

Trying to feel special, and he makes her feel that way.

But again, a reality check sets in

The guilt felt sinks in

The realization meets her face to face.

Hello, you are just the side chick.

The side chick's friend was there to listen and not judge.

All the while, hoping and praying that she would realize her place as only the side chick.

32

These Men

These men, as so many women, say

But could it be your whore-like ways

These men, as so many women, say

Could it be that they want a real woman?

Not a grown woman with childish ways

These men, as so many women, say

Could it be they are smarter than you believe, and your game is elementary?

These men, as so many women, say

Could it be that your twat is not worth what you think?

So, is it these men, or is it you?

33

These Scandals

The secrets that lie within all due to scandals from sins of sex and lies

The secrets that you hold and have forgotten to tell has others in prison in an unknown hell

The kids do not know who they are, all because of your sin of sex and lies

This betrayal has caused so many children to be prisoners with scars of unknown identity

Yet you wonder why they act the way they do.

Could it be because they genuinely do not know who they are?

You told them that one man was their father, yet he was not there when they were conceived.

Yet you wonder why they act the way they do

Mom, you do not know to whom they belong.

Your lifestyle then revealed your sin of sex, and now lies.

But you said my father was this man that I called dad all my life.

Now I find out that it was all a lie, but I now have this soul tie.

To someone who has treated me like I was his

But I am not his child by DNA, and now I will never know to whom I belong.

All because you were not yourself and you do not know

I have always looked up to you and dad, but this secret tears me up on the inside.

All because of this secret life of scandals that you lived of sex and lies.

All involved affected by the lies are clueless; because of what you were doing at the time.

Now our lives are built on the sins of sex and lies.

34

What Did I Do?

What did I do to hurt you?

That you would choose me to beguile

Making me think that a good woman you seek

When in reality, that was not the plan at all

You are doing a split.

Making others believe that you are with me

Yet what they do not see is that you never intended to be with me.

That is just what you wanted others to believe.

Your actions make me feel unworthy.

As you continue your prow of the same sex

Making me feel like I have always been too fat

It was not me at all.

It was your secret closet.

That you have never wanted to be exposed

Your craving for the hose, not the slit

While you continue to tell others, I do not want a big woman.

When in reality, big or small, neither is your desire.

Your lust is on fire for another type you desire

Why did you choose me to steal my years away?

While to others, you say, I would never be the one for you.

All I tried to do is be a friend.

Not be used as a pawn in your web of sin.

So, all I want to know is what did I do?

To be treated in this manner by you.

35

While the Wife's Away

While the wife's away on video chat, you play with another woman

I feel for her.

At the altar, you said, I do

She committed only to you.

When your wife is away, you decide to play.

On video chat, with another woman.

You think that your compliments draw women in by your words.

As if a tribute is all they need to enter your fidelity.

I feel for her, your wife, as she trusts in your loyalty.

She thinks of this man that put a ring on her hand will be committed only to her.

Yet on video chat, you play with another woman.

You have the pictures of the wedding day posted as your social media cover.

You and she appear happy on that day.

Yet while the wife is away on video chat, you play with another woman.

To work, she goes to help make your house a home.

However, on video chat, you play with another woman.

You say you want to chat, but the reality is you want video chat sex so you can jack off.

The woman you have trust you to be faithful to only her

But while the wife is away on video chat, you play with another woman.

Sorry, Bro, I am not the one. I do not need your tribute to my beauty.

I am better than the game you play.

I am disconnecting from you, and I am praying for your wife and you.

Stop this mess and be faithful to your wife like you promised before God and man.

To her, only you said I do, so be faithful.

That is what she and God are expecting from you.

36

What Silence Uncovers

When silence speaks, what will it say?

What will it uncover about the dark days?

From my youth, you stole many minutes, hours, and yes, days.

Monster, I cannot recover the time taken.

My mind was frozen on your acts of incest.

Yet my covering, my protector, still does not know.

Because I have been silent

Time after time, you invaded me.

I was afraid to cry out, so I kept silent.

Time and time again, you invaded my person.

These encounters should not have been my story. I was just a little girl.

But time and time again, you came and invaded my body with your touch, with your body parts.

You invaded me.

I cried from within, yet outwardly my cry was never heard.

I chose silence as my weapon because I did not know how the cry would be received.

Or if the cry would be believed.

So, I kept silent

Yet time and time again, you invaded my body with yours.

I hated your touch, your breath, your body, and your voice.

However, you were my family whom I was supposed to love.

But you invaded me time and time again.

Your invasion took me down a path that I should have never started to journey.

Sexual escapades with one after another

All because you attacked the younger me.

The growing me had to deal with the trauma of your touch, breath, body in mine, and your voice.

Others question my behavior as if I enjoy the ramifications of your actions, your invasion of me.

I was just a child, taken advantage of, hiding these ugly acts because you that scared me.

Your deeds caused me to feel unworthy.

Unworthy of the things that were promised to me because of your invasion.

You have the nerve to approach me still today with other forms of your lustful desire.

Although you know, now it would be to your disadvantage, because I am stronger now.

So, you cannot invade my body any longer, although your eyes try.

Now my silence speaks aloud, so don't stir up any of the memory.

I will blast with a loud voice of your intent to invade

Yes, my mind will speak aloud; it will uncover the monster; that is you.

So, you may want to leave my space before I shout aloud and reveal who you are, sick and perverted.

When my silence speaks, it will uncover the monster that you are.

The SOUL TIES

#Broken chains to freedom

37

Abstinence—My Body Armor

Yes, I protect my body.

Abstinence is the best way.

But if I decide to engage.

Yes, I will protect my body.

You say the latex makes you have an adverse reaction.

But suppose the non-use of it gives me an adverse reaction?

So, yes, I protect my body, wrap it up.

To you, my body is a depository for you to release yourself.

But to me, my body is unique and should only be given to my rib.

Not to you because you call this meeting an opportunity for you to make love to me

Something that you whisper in my ear to convince me that I need it and I should not do without it.

You say why should you deprive yourself of allowing me to make love to you.

When I ask you about the next steps in this pseudo-relationship, you say I do not want to discuss it.

Yet, you continue to discuss how I should let you reach a climax inside of me.

The more I tell you of my godly values,

You continue to respond with God made us this way and told me how much I need to fulfill the desire.

But, when I tell you of my desire to be in a committed relationship, you continue to say how you will not commit to a relationship because of our neighborhoods' distance.

Yet, for a rise in your nature and a release in a wet place, distance is not a problem.

Yet, I should take your pursuit of my body as a compliment that will cause me to burn with desire for you.

God knows you have a need you whisper over and over again in your pursuit of my good stuff.

Well, God knows my need for a committed relationship.

You say nothing about that need when I bring that up.

You often say, "I can't marry you; we do not get to spend any time together."

When I bring that up, you say our schedules do not permit.

We live too far from each other to see each other enough to say we are dating.

Yet, timing nor distance is a concern when you want to make love, as you call it.

My answer is still no because this house that I live in called my body is my responsibility to protect.

So yes, I protect my body with abstinence waiting for the committed one.

The one where schedules and distance between neighborhoods do not matter commitment will cause one to take the time necessary to build the relationship.

38

Back to a Virgin's State of Mind

Married for years

Used to the touch of my husband

Him in me, loving me.

The thrill of his thrust, the feel of his touch

Our embrace, our coming together in every way.

Time after time.

I was a virgin when he met me.

He deflowered me so patiently.

What do I do when I am used to intimacy, sex, and pillow talk?

Do I hang on to the memory of it?

The memory will cause me to thirst for the thrust he once gave

What does one do when they are used to the orgasmic thrill night after night?

How do you calm the rage inside?

Going from active to a dormant state of mind

I wonder did I make a mistake, should I have fought for who was mine

Now, I must refrain until the next time.

I am one again with a husband.

And that is if that event will occur again.

I am praying and fasting, yet the memory keeps coming to the forefront.

Causing my body to respond

Yet, there is no one here to quench my thirst or supply my needs.

So, back to a virgin's state of mind, I must try to go.

I try to embrace the place that I am in, to be content each day.

When the lights are turned down low, I am reminded of the memories, intimacy, and sex in that particular way.

That, I once enjoyed with my husband.

His thrust in and out of me comes to my mind as if we are face to face again.

What do I do?

I try to talk to other people with similar experiences, but mixed views I get.

Some will say to find someone to satisfy that need.

Others say, get over it and refrain, stop thinking about it; the feeling will pass.

No one seems to sympathize that this new single life is easier said than done.

People do not understand the struggle.

Nevertheless, I must do

What is necessary for me is to return to a pristine state of mind.

I must win the battle in my mind.

Mortify my flesh with its deeds

O Lord, help me!

With your help, I can return to a virgin's state of mind.

39

Did You Ask

How do you know what they want?

Did you ask?

Are you reading into it what you want?

Thinking, that is what they want

Setting yourself up for hurt

Do you like feeling like dirt?

Is this relationship worth your self-worth?

Why do you continue to play the victim?

When you allow this toxic system

To operate in your life

Causing you much strife.

You agonize over what you think

As you let your self-worth sink.

Do you know what their intentions are?

Again, I say, did you ask.

When a man says he does not want a commitment

Why do you stay, smitten?

Thinking it will turn around.

Those thoughts in your head are not sound.

Let it go

You are worth so much more.

Your days are numbered

So, stop wasting time.

Ask direct questions so that you'll find the answers that you need.

Stop wondering, agonizing, fretting, causing yourself the misery.

Whatever you want to know before you consider entering into this relationship and claiming he did not tell you that information.

When he reveals his character and you rant and rave of his deceit.

Ask yourself, did you ask?

40

I Know

I know what they have done.

I know that touch was not fun.

It was only supposed to be a date.

Instead, it turned out to be rape.

What just happened?

I said no.

But somehow, he thought I meant yes.

Why me?

He told me not to tell.

If I do, the consequences will be hell.

Mentally wounded caused me not to have the strength to fight.

How do I heal from this attack?

One day I heard about Jesus.

Then I began to see.

These chains of shame could no longer bind me.

Jesus' love for me helped to fade the memory.

Now I can share my story to let others know.

Jesus told me to rest in him because he sees, he cares, he knows.

41

I Was Designed to Be a Helpmeet

I am designed to be a helpmeet, not a provider.

When God took a rib out of the side of man

He called the women his helpmeet.

You seem to interpret the helpmeet status as

She provides the home.

She provides the car.

She provides the food.

She provides the upkeep.

She humbly submits

She provides the provision.

She pays the bills

She is an on-demand hooker.

She provides the credit.

She goes to work

If she gives all of that, why does she need you?

Unemotional love is not loving her.

She can achieve the same result from battery-operated devices.

If that is all she is getting from you is sex.

As long as the batteries stay charged, the same unemotional thrill can be achieved.

I am created to be a helpmeet, not the help.

So, let us work together and make it happen.

Let us love one another as it was intended to be.

Help in the Hebrew context meant support, assistance and aid.

Meet means mirror opposite, like our sexual organs.

She is internal, and he is external, opposite, but fit together.

We are perfectly designed to complement one another.

The man is the seed planter, and the woman is the incubator for the harvest.

Helpmeet means that we are both working together.

I can make this house a home.

But this marriage can only be a marriage if you do your part and I do mine.

God designed me to be your helpmeet.

42

This Level of Pain

One would think I am too young to experience this level of pain

To honestly know the difference between sunshine and rain.

You took my innocence with your power.

I still remember the day and the hour.

As you told me not to tell

About this private hell

I kept the secret in fear.

That secret cost me many tears.

I ask myself, why did you seek me.

Why no one said a word, not even a peep

For years, this secret I did keep.

I wanted so much for it to stop.

Week after week on my bed, you did plop.

I hated everything about you.

I wanted so much to shoot you.

I hated to hear the sound of your footsteps.

I hated to feel your breath.

When will this nightmare end?

I have been violated over and over again.

They wonder why I sit so isolated.

One day, my friend told me.

Jesus's love will mend my heart.

He will take away the pain.

He died for my shame.

He loves me dearly

He can help me through this stuff.

He taught me how to live.

And how to forgive.

Away you did go

I do not have to deal with you anymore.

Thank you, Jesus, oh how much I adore you

Jesus, you endued me with your power

I remember the day and the hour

When my change did come

Now my heart can hum.

I am free to be

All you have purposed for me

Walking in my destiny

I now can tell about my private hell.

Hopefully, this will aid others like me.

With hope, they too, like me, will be free.

43

My Dignity

My dignity is worth so much to me it is priceless.

My dignity means more to me than letting your bouncing motions inside me.

Yes, my dignity is worth more to me.

Then a quick, pleasurable encounter with you.

Your constant request for meetings with you in the dark place invading my space

An arrangement that means nothing more to you than a chance to get a wet release.

So, I say no to the high that could come from that pivotal moment.

My dignity means more to me than that moment in time-binding my mind.

Then your non-committed thrust inside.

So, yes, I choose my dignity.

44

Not Yours

What is this chauvinistic behavior?

Man, you are not my savior.

You have a wife

I am not sure of the direction of your strife.

She is to submit

I am single, so only to God's authority do I submit.

Every woman is not yours to control.

We are not tied to your soul.

Be careful how you treat me.

I am not yours

Let us get this straight; I am not your helpmeet.

There was only one rib taken from you.

The one you married is your helpmeet.

Our relationship is for business, ministry purposes only.

Watch how you handle me; talk to me.

I need to respect you, yes.

But I do not have to submit to you.

I am not your rib

Nor, am I the bone of your bone or flesh of your flesh

I am not yours.

45

This Mess

Your touch was amazing.

With passion, my emotions are blazing.

Awaiting the next time

While I live in constant regret all the time, I know you are not mine.

No, this is not an affair, single to single not sure why I can't be your woman publicly.

In reality, this will never be

This world of pretend.

Trapped in the act with you over and over again

How can we continue this sin?

I know it is wrong

However, it feels so right.

Amazing how once engaged

The passion is enraged.

Yet the guilt I feel.

Still, I continue to engage.

Your babe for those hours, minutes, and seconds

Knowing that I am not your type

Yet, you will not let me go.

You say the others you take out are just your friends, and you do not love any of them,

However, they are the ones that you make public appearances with often.

So, I allow you to use me while I seep more profound and in-depth in love with you.

With a fantasy that will never come true

You know it, and I know it.

How do I break free?

How do I go back to be me?

My heart needs an overhaul.

Only God can do that.

GOD!!!

Can you hear me? God, I need you?

GOD!!!

Can you hear me? My problem is a matter of the heart.

I do not know how to break free.

I know Jesus died for me.

I know this relationship is not right.

But for those hours, minutes, seconds, I feel so special.

But reality sets in, and I know I will never be His, and he will never be mine.

God!!!

Please hear my cry. I am ready.

To let him go

I am tired of this mess.

I want to be whole again; bless me, yes, God, even me.

To live your way, your way God.

46

Vices

Lord, help me not to depend

On the vices, I seem to use to mend.

My heart when in despair

When I know, you are the only one to repair.

Sometimes I sit and stare, wondering why

I use this avenue causing me to cry.

I yell for someone to help, but no one seems to care.

I turn to the vice while I sit and stare.

Wondering how this happened

As I search for a napkin

To wipe my tears

As I sit trembling with fear.

I then go on through the day.

Listening to the inner, I say,

"No more, this must stop."

I go for another fix from the vice.

I use to comfort to suffice.

What is eating away

At whom I am created to be day after day.

I have got to get to the core of my existence.

If my life will keep existing, and I begin living

God, I should have invited you into all areas of my life, both without and within.

Come in, Lord

Be Lord over every area.

Your Holy Spirit is here to lead and guide

I no longer must hide.

The stinky stuff that was once me

Jesus, you died to set me free.

No more torture from the shame

I am free to praise your name.

The Holy Spirit is my comforter.

Away with the vice

That tries to continue to entice.

I don't need you anymore.

Since I opened the door to my heart to let Jesus in

Now on him, I do depend.

He brought me out of a horrible pit.

Now in heavenly places, I do sit.

47

God Filled the Empty Places

The addiction is trying to fill the empty places.

For a moment, it appears to have done the trick.

Until you continue to need another fix

What is causing this urge of continuation?

Causing my body to crave more and more of this temporary fix.

The fix provides only moments of comfort to the empty place.

After the high of the fix dissipates, I understand that the empty place is still present now deeper.

This high, my heart it did not repair.

However, it is worse than the despair I feel.

No matter how much is being swallowed in the form of a pill

No matter how much is consumed as a meal

No matter the length on the climatic high

Whatever the vice that is chosen, it does not fill this void space the empty place.

What happened? When did this hole begin?

Several shovels were used to dig this deep place.

1. What they spoke about me started the digging

2. What they did to me dug deeper

3. What I began to accept inwardly caused the hole to go deeper

4. The comparison to others, my need to be confirmed, dug a deeper hole

5. What I believed about myself whispered in my ear by the wicked one dug deeper

6. The constant rejection dug more in-depth and deeper into my soul

Isolating me, making me feel lonely in a crowded room,

In a house full of people, yet alone.

I cry out to you, Lord help me, but maybe my cry is based on blame and shame, not on accountability for my actions.

I cry, wanting out, but my cry is so full of doubt.

Why does no one love me is what I think, I say

Pride, pity, and fear are still covering the hole.

I begin to search your Word, God, for the answer.

Seeking you, your kingdom first.

Forsaking my way, my fix

I ask for forgiveness for me and for me to forgive others.

You grant forgiveness, and then God, you forget what I am asking you to forgive.

Taking no thought for things, no more despair, no longer troubled, put a stop to worrying, replaced all with prayer and praise.

Now I can start on the road to my destiny, no longer misguided.

The direction is now clear.

Casting my cares on you, God no longer stressed.

God, you assured me that you would never forsake me or leave me alone, no longer lonely.

Resting in you, God, no longer tired, no more sleepless nights.

Angry sometimes but no longer letting the sun go down on my wrath,

Your peace compasses all my understanding

No longer sad because of your love for me, God; this is the day you made for me. Now I can rejoice and be glad.

No longer guilty.

Your Son Jesus died and bore the shame.

As You have resurrected Him and gave Him all power.

You resurrected and redeemed me, giving me restoration of all the years that have been consumed by addiction.

Depression had to flee when I gave up pride.

When I replaced fear with faith.

God, your light started to shine from inside me.

You filled the hole with the Holy Spirit; reminded me of all that you have given me, yes, an abundant life, full of joy and peace.

Thank you, God, for loving me and drawing me to fall in love with you.

No longer addicted to these vices, because of your sacrifice, there is now no condemnation.

I am free; chains now are broken because of my savior, my keeper, my sustainer, my lily of the valley, my bright and morning star, the lover of my soul, Jesus!!!

48

What Was Allowed

I know you thought I was too young to understand what went on behind closed doors.

A different man week after week

"Sit on my lap," he would say, as he caressed your daughter, my sister, and said, it was for play.

The green folded money that came out of his pocket.

It caused you to sit there like you were not aware of what he was doing.

The green folded money spoke louder to you than her cry.

What the love of money will allow

You wanted it bad enough to bow continually.

All you could see is the money you received

Never considering the damage, it was doing,

to your children.

The three of us have been scared deeply.

Yet these memories and nightmares don't say

You sacrificed anything for us in any way.

Yet you shout, I did my best for my girls.

Wow! what the love of money caused you to allow.

Jesus, who we came to know, made the ultimate sacrifice for all humankind.

I am so glad we know Him now.

Jesus Christ is the lover of our soul.

49

Seductive

Why is this sin so hard to resist?

They crave for it causes the body to insist.

On having an experience that feels good to the body

But to the soul, it places it deeper in a dark hole.

This sin warring against the spirit

But still, you continue to revisit it frequently.

Time and again, why did I start this sin

The craving for it grows and grows.

As it is continually satisfied

A piece of life continues to die.

You say to yourself; I need it.

Like an addict needs their next hit.

After the thrill is gone

Why, because of this sin?

This sin is committed in the body

Deposits and withdrawals being made

It is just fun, as one continues to engage each day.

Having different ones often makes some think that they are desirable

As you hide behind the rejection of never being accepted as the one

So, one tells themself they are wanted, they are desired, they are loved

Look at how they line up to have me

I allow them to feel my love, yet you are alone.

The seduction of the sexual immorality

The temptation is so strong, it is seductive

Luring your mind into thinking you need this high to survive

As one continues in this sin, the more they crave the high one gets.

When their body reaches the climactic moment

One shivers, shakes, and even screams at times

Only to realize your heart is still empty.

How can I escape this temptation to continue in this sin?

Continuing to relive it again and again

Look up to God; he can fill your heart with real love.

That only comes from above.

The enemy knows who you are, who God purposed you to be

You do not have to live that empty life anymore.

Let Him close each one of those doors.

You can come to Him. He is drawing you.

You can trust Him; He will keep you.

You can believe in Him; He has accepted you.

You can open up to Him; let Him fill you with His spirit.

Drink of His water and never be thirsty again

Remember He sent His Son, and He paid the price for your sin.

Believe what God says about you and who he says you can be.

It is He that gives you the strength to resist temptation.

It is He that gives you the power to live for Him.

Listen for His leading and let him fill every empty place with His love.

50

You Chose Him

Why did you choose him over us?

No matter what we said about him and despite the circumstances, you choose him.

Your so-called happiness means more.

This monster you adore.

He hurt sissy and me.

But you don't care.

You feel you need him more.

This monster you seem to adore.

I guess you are not enough for him.

So why do you stay

No matter what we say

To you, he means more than we do.

Wow, why do you choose him?

You left our dad because he cheated on you with another woman.

But this man cheats on you with your daughters.

Yet, you seem to adore.

My father knows of this wickedness, and we are leaving to live with him.

Bye, mom, do not be mad; remember, you chose him.

51

Broken Chains

These chains that had me bound

My cry to God released a sound.

A sound that said to God, I want to be free.

From these chains that are holding me

Sex, Lies, and Soul Ties

What a web of bondage these three did weave.

Chained up, Tied up, Wrapped up, I cry aloud, Lord deliver me!!!

I was fighting to get free of each struggle facing me, keeping me held by these chains.

Facing the fight alone, winning and losing through all this pain

Oh, if I only knew what I know now that Jesus broke the chains for me back on Calvary.

My praise will continue to be thank you, Jesus, for freeing me.

Yes, Jesus is the chain breaker!

The tragic incidents that caused this behavior

What I allowed to become my flavor

Whatever the case free me from this place

Let me forgive so I can live free from these chains holding me!

Your word says to give Jesus my life; His sacrifice has paid the price.

Yes, Jesus, take control for you, Jesus is the chain breaker!

Help me, Lord, to accept what you have done give up this sinful way that once was called fun!

I no longer have to carry these chains around, burdened and bound.

God's love for me has released what had me bound.

Jesus changed my heart, oh yes, I have decided.

I will follow the way that Jesus has provided!

Thank you, God I am not in this fight by myself.

You fixed the fight on Calvary, you sent your Son, and he died for me and everyone that will believe.

Thank you, GOD, for letting me see how you see me, free!

Yes, Jesus is the chain breaker!

God's Promise in his word promises me.

So, if the Son sets you free, you will be free indeed. John 8:36 (ESV)

Yes, Jesus is the chain breaker!

No matter when the chain links began to connect, wickedness thought it was prevailing.

God sent Jesus, and yes, his love is unfailing.

Yes, Jesus is the chain breaker!

His death on the cross broke the grip of sin; accept Jesus as your savior let His blood cleanse

So, no matter what life has or will bring, Jesus bared the guilt and the shame on the cross.

Oh yes, Jesus broke the chains so we would not be lost.

All power belongs to GOD.

So, by His Power, we are set free.

His saving power breaks all the power of the enemy.

When we trust, hope, and believe, we are free.

Letting go of what is linking willing to forgive to stop sinking

God heals the heart, strengthens the body, prospers the soul, and gives peace to the mind.

If you will resist the temptation, your escape is made.

The Promise of his word says:

For God will break the chains that bind his people Isaiah 9:4 (TLB)

I release you today from the chains on your hands Jeremiah 40:4 (ESV)

O Lord, you have loosed my chains.

For I am the Lord your God, who brought you out of the land of Egypt so that you would be slaves no longer; I have broken your **chains** so that you can walk with dignity. Leviticus 26:13 (TLB)

13 Then they cried to the Lord in their troubles, and he rescued them! **14** He led them from the darkness and the shadow of death and snapped their chains. Psalm 107: 13- 14 (TLB)

So Christ has made us free. Now make sure that you stay free and don't get all tied up again in the chains of slavery….. Galatians 5:1 (TLB)

God sent Jesus his Son, because of his redeeming love for humankind, Jesus went to the cross with a made up mind.

Jesus was wounded for me, beaten for me, suffered for me, his bloodshed for me broke every chain just for me.

Well, really for us all

Yes, Jesus is the chain breaker!

www.ingramcontent.com/pod-product-compliance
Lightning Source LLC
Chambersburg PA
CBHW021115080526
44587CB00010B/526